From Congress *to the* Brothel

A Journey of Hope, Healing, and Restoration

LINDA SMITH

Founder
Shared Hope International

ISBN 978-0-9896451-3-3

Cover and text art by Hampton Creative

© 2014 Shared Hope International

Printed in the United States of America.

Shared Hope International
P.O. Box 65337
Vancouver, WA 98665
www.sharedhope.org

CONTENTS

ACKNOWLEDGEMENTS

Shared Hope has celebrated 16 years as an organization. For the first eight years, I regularly resolved to write this book. But with each passing year, new Homes of Hope were started, with more girls needing attention, more girls escaping years of slavery, more girls beginning to re-build their lives. I simply never felt I had enough time.

Without a few determined people, this book would not exist.

Each year, Dr. Dale Berkey would gently prod me with the suggestion that it was time. God had done so much ... shouldn't we tell people about it? Without the help of Dale and his great staff at BBS & Associates, I would likely still be saying "Next year will be fine!" Thank you, Dale, and the Berkey team.

Now eight years later, we are republishing this little book with the addition of testimonies of lives saved through our ministry — some testimonies of children who came to our homes 16 years ago.

A special thanks to Shared Hope's family of supporters and volunteers who kept encouraging me with the reminders that it is important for the future of our ministry to tell of what God has done through us to give life to the girls we serve.

This book would look pretty rough without the editing of several Shared Hope staff members. Shared Hope and I have been blessed with an outstanding Board of Directors over the years. The constant comfort of knowing that I am not alone in the fight, but rather standing with strong men and women of God has given me the courage to take bold steps into dark places.

Without the other half of my memory reminding me of how things really were, some of this book would not have been written. I would not have been able to remember some of the intimate thoughts and little details my husband Vern recalled. Once again, God has reminded me of how this humble man completes me and makes all that I am able to do so much better.

INTRODUCTION
See for Yourself

A 13-year-old girl crouched in a dark corner on the dusty floor, her hair dirty and tangled, her eyes hollow and lifeless. Raw sewage flowed through an uncovered ditch on the other side of the thin brothel wall. The scent of a hundred men clung to her small frame. Her expression revealed total desperation. This was not a look that said, "Please help me." This was a look that said, "I am doomed forever, beyond help, beyond hope."

It was as if God Himself whispered in my ear, "Touch her for Me." My hand suddenly weighed 90 pounds. I froze. My head felt light from holding my breath. I could taste the stench. Would the filth make me vomit? Would I contract a deadly disease by just breathing the air? I wanted to leave my hands tucked safely in my pockets, with my arms pressed tightly to my sides to avoid brushing up against anything. But I couldn't ignore the internal voice: "Touch her for Me."

Obediently, I reached out and touched her dirty, frail shoulder. In that moment, my life changed. At my soft touch, the desperate little girl fell into my arms with gratitude. My simple gesture overwhelmed her because she was so utterly unloved in this world.

Suddenly, the stench evaporated. She didn't appear filthy. She appeared beautiful. She was not worthless. She was a child of God.

I raised my eyes to look around the small room. Dozens of girls sat around me — all trapped in the same living horror. They were part of India's sex industry — slaves locked in cage-like conditions existing to satisfy the sexual appetites of the next man wanting to buy them.

A man entered the room. He tapped a girl on the shoulder, summoning her to service another man. She followed obediently. Again, my stomach turned — only this time it wasn't because of the stench. Who could do this to a child?

One of the worst brothel districts in the world can be found on Falkland Road in Bombay. I passed hundreds of stalls along the narrow street. Each contained dozens of girls. Each girl sold by her owner to 20 to 40 men per day. I felt sick.

Men strolled past the stalls, like window shoppers, looking and choosing their product.

How could I return to the safe halls of Congress as a U.S. Representative knowing this little girl, and thousands like her, live every day with the fear of beatings, starvation, and rape? Men locked them in small, dark rooms between visits from "buyers." Men used their haggard little bodies 20 to 40 times a day. These were not women. They were just school-aged girls. They were not there by choice. They had been sold into slavery by desperate parents, or abducted and spirited away by masters of the sex slave industry.

No, I had to do something. But what?

CHAPTER 1

As Much
as
I Love You

Nothing in my travels, nothing I'd heard in gut-wrenching testimony on Capitol Hill had come close to the quiet nightmare I witnessed those first nights in the brothel district of Mumbai. I stood there on Falkland Road feeling completely horrified and helpless.

I represented Washington State in the House of Representatives from 1994 to 1999. I lived and fought in the congressional trenches making tough decisions under pressure. Then a phone call changed my life.

Due to a tight schedule, my staff had limited my phone calls, with a few exceptions. David Grant's call was one of them.

A mission's director for the Assemblies of God in south Asia, he told me about the unspeakable horrors in Mumbai. I had never talked to Mr. Grant before that day, but he had heard me speak at the Assembly of God denomination's international convention.

I stood with phone to ear and listened — and listened and listened. I listened for 40 minutes. I didn't understand everything he said. This passionate missionary, connected to a group called Bombay Teen Challenge, spoke of something new to me. His words appalled and riveted me at the same time.

He spoke of girls kept in cages, women living literally as slaves. He spoke of the horrors of the sex trafficking industry.

"Come to India and see for yourself," he implored.

The idea filled me with trepidation, but something in me wanted to confirm his story. Was he exaggerating? Suddenly, perhaps miraculously, a five-day window of availability appeared in my normally hectic schedule. Within a few weeks, I was on a plane bound for Bombay.

Members of Congress address human rights atrocities around the world, but absolutely nothing compared to the nightmare I saw in Bombay. Nothing prepared me for the horror these children live in.

Mr. Grant's phone call opened my eyes. The trip to Bombay changed my life.

Noxious fumes stole my breath the moment
I stepped off the plane. Mobs of people bumped
into me. They pushed and shoved one way and
then the next.

MR. GRANT'S PHONE CALL OPENED MY EYES. THE TRIP TO BOMBAY CHANGED MY LIFE.

Diesel, urine, and incense mingled in the humid air
until I could taste the stench and my eyes watered.
Doubt flooded my mind. Yet, there I was in Bombay's
chaotic airport. In India, women are perceived as
property and politicians as corrupt. Therefore, I was
a double suspect.

What could I accomplish here?

Several men, from the same ministry as Mr. Grant,
were awaiting my arrival and would be my hosts
for the duration of my visit. One of them was K.K.
Devaraj, the founder of Bombay Teen Challenge.

"Where do you want to go?" he asked.

"I want to see what I came to see," I answered
matter-of-factly.

The men looked at me as if I were crazy. It was the
middle of the night. But I persisted. Brothels conduct
most of their business at night, so this seemed to me
like the best time to witness the degradation I had
heard about.

They took me to Falkland Road.

I can still smell it.

A woman stepped out of an alleyway — or what I thought was an alleyway. It turned out to be a street paved with brothel stalls, a hell on earth. Ruthless brothel owners prostitute thousands of young girls here to satisfy the throngs of men who come to buy sex from the vulnerable.

I followed the woman into the darkness. The stench stole my breath. I did not know how to relate to these girls, some near the age of my 11-year-old granddaughter. I left that night in sorrow. It wasn't until I returned the next night that I finally mustered enough courage to approach the girls.

Shobona, a Teen Challenge outreach worker (once a brothel manager, before coming to know the Christian God's unconditional love for her and the girls she once brutalized), asked me to pray for the girls. That was the moment I reached out to touch that wispy little girl. Feelings of helplessness were once again upon me.

Days passed. I bargained with God. "I'm doing a lot of good as a policy-maker," I told Him. "I'm helping millions of people. I can do far more good by staying in public policy, fighting for the unborn child, or even raising the money needed to help these girls. God, You trained me in business, policy, and politics. How could I justify devoting my life to one little girl in a distant, dark corner of the world — or even a handful like her?"

But God gently nudged me to see things differently. "I love her as much as I love you," He reminded me. "She is precious to Me."

God used that desperate, foul-smelling little girl to send me down a remarkable path. Shared Hope International was born out of that experience. As I discovered the astonishing scope of the problem, my decision became clear. I would leave politics and devote my life to intervening on behalf of women and children bound in sexual slavery.

Today, by God's great grace, we have developed a worldwide network of safe houses and services for women and children trapped in forced prostitution, torture, and abuse in India, South Africa, Nepal, Jamaica — and even the United States.

Women and children rescued from sexual slavery are victims. They lack self-worth and the skills needed to make a new start in life. Many still fear for their lives. Many have fled forced abortions and face their pregnancy alone. Others battle deadly diseases with nowhere to turn for help, and no money to seek medical care.

Our safe houses are called Homes of Hope. Through partnerships with local organizations, our homes give these precious girls a safe, nurturing community to regain physical and spiritual health. We feed them. We give them medical care, housing, schooling, job training, and counseling. Some homes consist of several safe houses, while others consist of an entire village. No matter the size, they all provide educational and vocational training that offer the once enslaved hope and freedom for a better future.

I went from Congress to the brothel — and have never looked back.

CHAPTER 2

Trail
of
Tears

Gina lived unaware of her family's poverty. Her simple life in the Nepalese village revolved around the annual cycles of planting and harvest, monsoon and drought.

Little Gina has only wisps of fuzzy memories from the night that changed her life. She can close her eyes and taste the strong tea her uncle gave her to drink. The bitter taste lingers. The nightmare had begun.

Gina awoke thousands of miles from the familiar rice fields, startled into reality by choking odors — diesel, urine, and incense. Her eyes opened slowly, and she stared into the face of evil. She never imagined anything like this.

Gina remained in her quiet hell for four soul-scarring years. She was a slave to every man who paid for her. Her captors laid an endless debt on her for the cost of her initial travel and her ongoing lodging, meals, clothing, and so-called care. But this little girl fought for freedom. Determined, she scrimped and saved to pay off the contrived debt even though her captors increased it daily.

HER ONLY CONSTANT IS FEAR. SHE LONGS TO RUN, BUT CAN'T.

Trafficked women call journeys such as Gina's the "trail of tears." The terrifying journey often begins in Nepal. Unsuspecting young girls in villages and the countryside are taken from their families, sold, or lured with a promise of a job and a better life in India.

Snatchers sometimes drug the girls before traveling often 1,000 miles or more. Then a broker sells them to a brothel owner.

What a shock! What fear for a nine-year-old girl. Gina did not know where she was. She could not understand the language. She felt lost, alone, and confused. Then began the steady stream of men — the absolute horror of days and nights and man after man after man. These little girls are gang-raped, beaten, and emotionally manipulated. Her only constant is fear. She longs to run, but can't. The feeling is impossible to describe.

Gina's trail of tears is repeated thousands of times over. Why do people want to harm a precious young child? These little girls should be playing with dolls, not ravaged by a long line of selfish, soulless men.

Young Gina is one of the first girls I met during my initial trip to Bombay. Her story shocked me.
Still, my negotiations with God continued. "Look, I'm a businesswoman, a policy-maker. None of this seems to fit. Are You sure You didn't intend to call someone in the next office?"

No, it didn't make sense. But I was the one there.

The next evening, still in shock — still completely overwhelmed — I went with K.K. Devaraj to a little church he had set up for the prostituted girls, a makeshift congregation right there on Falkland Road. Brothel owners would pull the girls out for 15 minutes at a time, right in the middle of the service.

I looked around. Many of them were teens at most. Some young women held babies. Their eyes were dark and lifeless. Some were obviously sick. Lice crawled visibly in their hair. The smell, as always, overwhelmed the environment.

Yet, these girls were praising God. They expressed their love for the Lord. They would return from being with a client and resume worship. This was not the life these girls and young mothers asked for. They were slaves.

The missionary asked me to say a few words. And then he said a funny thing. He referred to me as their "sister."

In that moment it struck me: we were indeed fellow females — sisters in Christ Jesus. I stood and spoke from my heart. I told these vulnerable girls that God has a big family, and that He had brought us together.

When asked to pray, emotions once again flooded me. I felt repulsed. Honestly, I did not want to touch those girls. "I am not going to touch you," I thought to myself over and over again — all the while begging of the Lord, "Why me?"

But I began to pray for them. When I pray for a sister back home, I often put my arms around her and hold her tightly against me. The Holy Spirit challenged me to reach out to this little sister, and as I reached out and touched her, she fell into me. I can still feel her frail body, her heart beating against mine, as if it were just yesterday. Suddenly, a heartfelt longing to help these girls overwhelmed me. I had to rescue them from the chains of this life and offer them safe refuge.

K.K. Devaraj founded Bombay Teen Challenge to minister to street boys — the forsaken little fellows who sleep on the streets and spend their days begging. He had set up facilities for their care and had devoted his life to these desperately needy little ones.

I realized that just as K.K. Devaraj had been called to the boys, God burdened my heart for the girls. I didn't know exactly what it meant or what it might require, but at that moment, I overwhelmingly knew it was my calling.

In those first five days in India, I prayed fervently, burdened for the girls. I asked a lot of questions and did a lot of research. I pursued the possibility of establishing homes for the girls on property owned by the Indian Christian leaders of Teen Challenge. I looked at establishing safe houses for them to flee to right in the city. I found out about rent, down payment on a lease (expensive in that culture: a hefty $10,000), and figured out the costs of staffing, food, and medical care. I drew from my business and management skills, developing a basic plan of action.

I CAN STILL FEEL HER FRAIL BODY, HER HEART BEATING AGAINST MINE, AS IF IT WERE JUST YESTERDAY.

I needed to make two important calls: one to my husband and the other to a wealthy businesswoman friend. These two phone calls would determine my course — abandon this crazy idea or forge ahead.

If I can reach them, I had decided — if they say yes and I know I can get cash — that will be my answer. I will know we are supposed to get started.

My husband Vern answered right away. He barely said hello before I spilled out all my fears and frustrations on this dear man over the phone. I tried to explain what I was seeing and feeling. When he finally spoke, his words were few but clear, "We have to do this, don't we, Linda?"

My friend picked up her own phone on the first ring. That never happens. A housekeeper normally answered the phone. Furthermore, it seemed unlikely to me that she would give toward such a concept.

This friend was a major political supporter who was gunning for me to leave the House of Representatives and run for governor of the State of Washington. It didn't make sense for her to say yes to a project that would take my time and attention away from politics.

I told her about the horrors on Falkland Road. I said I wanted to start a home for girls escaping the slavery of being prostituted.

"Once you get them," she asked me, "what are you going to do with them?"

"I don't know yet, but at least we can give them freedom. *Will you help?*"

She asked me how much I needed. "$25,000 to start," I said. This would establish the first Homes of Hope, a safe house, and run it for a year.

"How much of that do you want from me?" she asked.

"All of it," I replied.

That was Tuesday. By Thursday, I had the money in hand. We opened the first Homes of Hope with Bombay Teen Challenge within a few weeks.

I did not set out to establish Shared Hope International. I didn't even want to go to India at first. Something within prompted me to go. Once there, the situation overwhelmed me. It was so much bigger than me. I felt too old, too tired to take on such incredible work. How could I cope with a problem of such magnitude? Then God reminded me of a valuable lesson: God doesn't rely on my will. He just asks that I show up ... and obey that urge to step forward. God uses that willingness to accomplish valuable things.

I had no idea what the next step would be. My friend's question, "What are you going to do with the girls?" rang in my ears. But God had asked me to "just show up," and that was exactly what I was determined to do.

CHAPTER 3

Mud,
Straw,
Dung

I take action whenever faced with need. It's what brought me to India. I can't just hear about a problem. I must do something about it. And I couldn't witness the horror that I saw on Falkland Road without doing whatever I could to help.

But this was a difficult thing to act on. I struggled deeply.

I wrestled with the culture. I wrestled with my own insufficiencies. I wrestled against time. I had to move quickly to set the plan in motion before my plane returned to D.C. Only a few days remained. Despair crept into my thoughts.

As I looked over the countryside just outside of Bombay, contemplating how to set up the first safe house for the girls, something caught my eye. Odd-looking thatched houses dotted the fields. I asked about them and learned they belonged to groups of families who were brick-makers, an actual societal class in India, handed down from generation to generation. If you were born into a family of brick-makers, then that was your caste. You became a brick-maker, as would your sons, daughters, and grandchildren.

Bricks are an important building material in India and are always in great demand. But as I learned that day, brick-making is dirty work, requiring a blend of patience and back-bending labor. Brick-makers work long hours gathering mud, straw, and dung. They mix it together in trenches, form the bricks one at a time, bake them in brick kilns, and then set them in the sun where the bricks season further, becoming hardened — and useful.

And in that very moment, I had a clear picture in my mind.

God reminded me how the whole of my life — up to this very point — had prepared me for what He was now asking of me.

My life was Romans 8:28 in action: "And we know that in all things God works for the good of those who love him, who have been called according to his purpose."

God doesn't just work the good stuff for good! Sometimes, it requires the mixing of some tough stuff — the mud and the straw and the dung —

to make something useful.

I began to think back over my life. I started working pretty young. I love to work. I am a natural entrepreneur. As an 11-year-old, I used these skills aggressively and started my own business, going door to door and doing chores for senior ladies in my neighborhood. My family wasn't affluent, so I needed to work, and I quickly learned the value of work.

GOD REMINDED ME HOW THE WHOLE OF MY LIFE — UP TO THIS VERY POINT — HAD PREPARED ME FOR WHAT HE WAS NOW ASKING OF ME.

Soon, I began thinning pear trees in orchards, picking fruit, working at a fruit stand, cleaning houses, taking in ironing, and working in a day care center, among other things. Working was my way to get the things other kids had.

But when I was a young teen, my mother became ill. She spent years battling heart disease and cancer. I had four younger siblings, and when my older sister married and left home, the others were often left to my care. Suddenly, I found myself with a lot of added responsibility.

I was an honors student and drove myself to get good grades in school. Every moment of my day was spent between school, work, and home. I started early and worked late. At times, it exhausted me.

Those early years served me well as I developed a successful career as a tax consultant, built on long work hours and determination.

Looking back, it is as if I picked up a lot of straw and did my fair share of back-bending labor.

So why would I add the dirty mud of politics to my happy and relatively successful life?

Two things led me to run for office.

I was not politically involved until my husband became a pro-life activist overnight. One Saturday he came home from a men's breakfast at our church and immediately sought me out. He very deliberately explained how the speaker that morning had taught from the Bible about how God viewed the unborn. Vern then made the statement that changed our life: "Linda, I prayed this morning and made a commitment to God that even if there were only one man left standing, that for me and my family, we would fight for life." He proceeded to become the president of the local pro-life group.

The second thing that got this businesswoman's attention was the Washington State Legislature's vote that doubled my business taxes!

So I went into politics — the mud! I survived eight political races. By the grace of God, I was successful, but each of those campaigns held its share of nasty accusations, personal attacks, and crushing negativity. It's hard to stand up and brush that off over and over and over again. There was a lot of ugly mud. And mud is sticky — it doesn't clean up so easily.

It hurts to add — but I must — I was molested periodically as I grew up. I spent years running from some people in my life. There is still healing going on in my relationships and with members of my family. It was only a couple of years ago when another family member and I came to the point of revealing to each other what had happened to us and discovered that our experiences had been tragically similar.
People hide things for years. But when those issues re-surface, you are forced to face the same raw pain and heartache, just as real and still so tender.

And in that first encounter with the girls in Bombay, I remember not wanting to face that — face the horrors of abuse they had been through and replaying the nightmare of those I had suffered as well.

I, too, had been penned, blocked, lured in a way — awful memories that still give me shivers.

Yet God painted a new picture in my mind. It was as if I were stooped over and struggling, carrying all of this junk — guilt, fear, awful memories, distractions — all piled high on my shoulders.

Yet as I carried all of the mess in my life, "the gunk," God gently reminded me:

The strongest bricks have manure in them.

That "manure" — the experiences I would consider the very worst in my life — those were the very experiences that had made me ready. "All things work together for the good." Not just the good things. All things.

Then I saw myself standing on a pile of bricks. I was no longer struggling, and I couldn't smell the dung, the rancid mixture that had gone into making the bricks. Now, I realized, He was holding my chin up so I could see. He had lifted me up — far above the trenches filled with mud and straw and dung.

MOLDED IN GOD'S OWN HAND, BAKED UNDER THE HEAT AND PRESSURE OF LIFE — IT HAD BECOME A PLATFORM FOR ME TO MINISTER FROM.

The mud and straw and manure of my life had become something new and usable and strong. Molded in God's own hand, baked under the heat and pressure of life — it had become a platform for me to minister from.

And let me tell you something: you can see so much farther standing on a pile of bricks than you can while stooped over, struggling with their weight on your back!

That thought changed me forever. I still might struggle with how to do it, but no more questioning, no more wondering "What if I made a mistake?"

He drew a line there for me as surely as He sent me to Congress without me even filing for office. Yes, you read that right: I did not decide to run for Congress, but was elected after a spontaneous 10-day grassroots write-in campaign that was started while I was out of town on vacation. More than 40,000 people wrote my name on their ballot in the September 1994 primary election, swamping the incumbent. I knew this was a miracle that only God could carry off. No mortal can organize 40,000 people to do anything, and do it right, in such a short time!

Yet as it turned out, those years were not the point of my life story, but rather a valuable springboard to this ministry. I look back now and realize I never would have known many of the people who are helping us in this ministry today if it weren't for my years in Congress. And I couldn't effectively influence laws that impact those enslaved if it weren't for my years on Capitol Hill.

I'm not making it happen — I know I'm nothing on my own — but because of what God has brought me through, I can be a catalyst. I can let God use the straw and mud and dung to make something useful. Something strong. If I just show up.

If I'm just obedient to God's calling, by taking the steps He asks me to take and seizing the opportunities He places before me, the grace He pours through me is limitless!

That day in Bombay, India, I decided to be obedient. I was going to help prostituted girls find new life. I was going to help them make bricks from their own sad straw, their own awful mud, and the terrible, tragic dung of their lives.

POOJA AND SHOBA

CHAPTER 4

Homes
of
Hope

Ganga was a sweet little girl, full of wonder and innocence, blessed with a beautiful round face and almond-shaped eyes. Ganga's early days as a child were happy. Then suddenly, all of that changed.

Ganga's father asked her to take the trip with him to sell wares in the city. The invitation excited her because she had never ridden on a train.

When she got to the city and turned around in the big train station, her father was gone. Frightened, she began to cry. A friendly old man said she could come to his house and his wife would care for her until they could find her father. Taking a welcome drink from him, Ganga went with this man, thankful for his kindness.

She awoke in confusion and terror. She had no idea where she was. A desperate family member had sold her into sexual slavery.

Ganga woke in a tiny dark room surrounded by loud street noises, strong smells, and voices yelling in unfamiliar languages. Cruel brothel owners kept her locked in this dark room for months. The door opened only twice a day, a little food was slid through, and then darkness returned. One more year, and this little girl would be ready for their evil use.

Her owner tortured, abused, and threatened to kill her if she didn't allow the throngs of filthy men to have their way with her at all hours of the day and night. Many days, the brothel owner forced her to have sex with 20 men or more. She faced physical danger and the threat of fatal diseases, including HIV/AIDS.

Beautiful little Ganga became a shell of her once happy self, existing in the darkness and agony of a world we cannot imagine. Day in and day out, Ganga lived in her small room, lock and chain on the outside of the door — a door which only opened for the next man who came to abuse her.

After a couple of years, the owners of the brothel became comfortable with Ganga. They knew she was too broken and hopeless to resist them. They stopped keeping a close eye on her every move.

But obviously, they did not know this little girl. One night she escaped, fleeing home to her village.

Still, her heartbreak was incomplete. Her own family

rejected her — a constant reality for victims such as Ganga. Her family wanted nothing to do with a "prostitute."

In hopelessness, Ganga wandered the streets alone. She had no money. No family. What would she do for food or shelter? How could she survive?

I believe little Ganga is one of the first reasons God asked me to "just show up" in India.

There have been so many other beloved girls since that time, but even if there hadn't been ... even if Ganga had been the only little girl who took refuge in our newly established Homes of Hope ... I still would have felt 100% certain of this calling.

As this broken little girl wandered the streets, God intervened — the first of many divine interventions to happen in our work. An outreach worker from our Homes of Hope safe house invited Ganga to the Bombay Teen Challenge church service, and Ganga heard about a God who loved her.

That worker brought Ganga to our Homes of Hope, where she received much needed medical attention and shelter. For months, the frail and battered girl trusted no one.

But through the constant, tender care of other women in the safe house, Ganga realized she was finally free from the "bad people." And more importantly, Ganga came to understand that a great big God loved her — regardless of her past.

Ganga found hope. She found safety. She found healing.

GANGA CAME TO UNDERSTAND THAT A GREAT BIG GOD LOVED HER — REGARDLESS OF HER PAST.

And Shared Hope International found its purpose. As each new victimized girl or enslaved young mother with an endangered child found her way to our doorstep, we further realized the scope of the need. We became determined to take a three-pronged approach:

Prevention — From my first walk down Falkland Road, I knew that prevention would have to be a vital part of our work. Today, efforts to confront and prevent child prostitution and sex trafficking remain a clear focus of Shared Hope International.

Rescue — As in Ganga's story, rescue could be more adequately described as intervention. We have a presence in the brothel districts, at sex tourist destinations, and at the other end of telephone hot lines. We also are visible through mobile HIV/AIDS clinics and food distribution centers. In many cities, once word gets out about a safe place to flee from their captors, girls will come, or risk escaping, to stop yet another beating or forced abortion. The God-given love of a mother for her unborn baby is a powerful motivator.

Restoration — We are one of only a few programs in the world offering long-term care for sex slaves through our secure Homes of Hope shelters.

We are readily available and deeply committed to women and children who are looking to escape the horrors of their slavery, offering hope, healing, and a chance for a better future.

At the beginning, we had our work cut out for us. We had a lot to learn.

But in those first few months at the Homes of Hope, it was thrilling to see progress. To watch hurt and heartache turn to hope. To see smiles on precious faces hardened and aged by years of absolute horror and degradation. To witness the process of brick-building — and know what a beautiful new "view of the world" these women had in store!

One night, I hosted a party for all the young women in the safe houses, bringing a gift for each of the rescued young women. I brought each one a wristwatch — symbolizing the gift of time.

That, in fact, is what we had given back to these women. While slaves, each moment was determined for them by the will of another. While you and I might take each hour for granted, these women recognize the gift of time ... and it was now theirs to fill.

That night, we celebrated! We had a wonderful opportunity to talk and laugh together. But one young woman sat quietly in the corner. Finally, I asked her what was wrong. Her voice was filled with despair as she answered: "I miss my baby."

A few years earlier, **Shoba** had given birth to a daughter, Pooja, in a small Nepali village. Pooja would be the only girl Shoba and her husband would keep.

Due to extreme poverty, most Nepali families cannot afford the cost of raising girls. Boys produce more and cost less; therefore, a mother rejoices at the arrival of a boy and weeps when a girl is born. Girl babies are often left for dead or killed by their families. To many Nepalese, the act of killing baby girls is pure economics.

In this culture, women are regarded as a commodity. They can be traded, bought, and sold by their husbands and families. Often wives are banished from their homes because their husband's family has decided to marry another woman who brings a larger dowry or belongs to a higher caste, or because she simply does not produce the prized son.

This was Shoba's fate. Stripped of her family, her precious daughter, and her possessions, Shoba was transported to a brothel 900 miles south in Bombay. She slept on a single dirty mattress in a room infested by filth and disease. An elevated board, about the size of a door, hung within the brothel stall. It served as her bed and the place where men abused her. Underneath, Shoba kept her small bundle of belongings, all she owned in the world.

Shoba worked with one goal in mind: earning enough rupees to pay off her debt to the brothel. She often serviced up to 45 clients a day.

Despair threatened to erase Shoba's hope of ever seeing her daughter Pooja. Day in and day out, there seemed no end to her violent existence. Fear of being beaten, tortured, or raped kept Shoba from escaping the bondage of the brothel. Yet in her heart, she longed for nothing more than to simply embrace her daughter one more time.

Then one day, some of the "sisters" in the brothel told Shoba about a church in the center of Bombay that perhaps could help her. Shoba made her way to the church and met outreach workers there.

Once the outreach workers were able to secure Shoba's freedom from the brothel, they immediately took her to the Homes of Hope safe house. At the safe house, it wasn't long before Shoba began to talk about her "baby," Pooja.

As she explained her grief to me, my joy at giving the gifts and celebrating with the women turned to despair and heartache. How on earth could I find Shoba's little girl in a vast, strange place like the country of Nepal?

On the flight home, I felt deeply discouraged.

What can I do? The thought plagued me. Like the children of Israel, staring down the giants of Canaan, I felt as small as a grasshopper beside this overwhelming evil. Again, I cried out to God for guidance.

"Just show up," He whispered in my ear.

Not long after arriving at home, I got a call. Ten of our young ladies had returned to Nepal and were living in our new home there. Shoba was one of them.

My mother's heart wept at what I thought was a futile attempt to get close to her daughter.

What I was soon to learn lifted my spirits and gave me new hope and joy in knowing the God of miracles. Some of the Homes of Hope team in Nepal had taken Shoba out to her former village. They found the house she had lived in, and after surveying the area for a while, they soon caught a glimpse of Pooja. This was a dangerous situation for Shoba, so the team returned to the safe house. We discovered that Pooja was living in the village as a "housemaid" — actually just another way of being held as a slave in that culture — with her father and stepmother. Clearly she was a commodity to them and would inevitably meet the same fate dealt to her mother. With that, arrangements were made by the team to secure Pooja, and within days she was reunited with her mother at Shared Hope's Homes of Hope.

"JUST SHOW UP"

Behind our protective doors, a beautiful Nepali woman tightly embraced her eight-year-old daughter for the first time in two years. They shed tears of joy and relief. After what seemed like an impossible feat, the mother and daughter were together once again.

As a teenager, Pooja has been attending private school in preparation for college. She dreams of a future now. She has the chance to fulfill her heart's desires. It is all within reach.

Shoba is a strong leader, actively involved in our Homes of Hope ministry by reaching out to women still in bondage in the red light districts and training other survivors to do the same. Shoba has become a vital part of our program. She is proof of how God can fully restore a life!

"Just show up," God keeps reminding me. "Let Me do the rest."

And without fail, He does.

CHAPTER 5

Standing
on the
Bricks

Sometimes, it's not enough just to be rescued. Ganga, Shoba, and Pooja showed us this. It's what happens next that is most important.

We quickly realized that what these women needed was to be given purpose for the day. Although they had been given freedom, they had no idea what to do with it.

So we ventured into new territory for the women in our care at the Homes of Hope. We launched a personal and economic development program called the "Women's Investment Network," or WIN. Through WIN, we gave each of the women the chance to learn an occupation. Before long, we saw an amazing difference. Suddenly, the women were awakening each morning with a sense of value and dignity. For the first time, they had more to offer than just their bodies.

Springing from this new sense of purpose for the day was renewed hope and healing — and purpose for tomorrow.

Our outline was simple: get well first, become mentally and physically stable, and then start building your future. We knew this would not be a short-term ministry. We were now family. These girls were ours for life!

Today, our WIN program continues to allow women in the Homes of Hope ministry to build lives of discipline and dignity. They work in businesses located on campus, ranging from a bakery to a pre-school, from jewelry-making to floral sales to a hospitality center. Each woman takes a turn at the different occupations and is given a percentage of her sales to spend on her individual needs and her child's needs, as well as to save toward independent living. More importantly, she is given a chance to succeed, to find worth, and to value her own abilities.

SHE KNEW THE AWFUL TRUTH: HER MOTHER HAD SOLD HER INTO THE FIJIAN SEX INDUSTRY.

WIN has worked so well in India, we've begun to use it in our other Homes of Hope established around the world. Poverty is a major cause of women being trafficked into sexual slavery, so this strategy — providing victims with skills and the means to create their own economic sustainability — helps diminish the risk of re-victimization. Soon after launching Shared Hope, we learned that sexual slavery is seen as a "no way out" condition, typically passed down from generation to generation. But now, Shared Hope is working to break that cycle, giving these women hope through the WIN program.

Natalie will tell you it saved her life.

This young girl watched in horror through the back window of a taxi as her mother, counting a wad of cash, disappeared from sight in a cloud of dust. As her home slipped further and further from view, the school girl glanced at the old man sitting beside her and was overwhelmed by a sense of betrayal. She knew the awful truth: her mother had sold her into the Fijian sex industry.

Natalie is one of thousands of Fijian girls sold into prostitution each year. Tourism is popular on the exotic island, bringing multitudes of European, Australian, and American men eager to buy young girls for a few moments of perverse pleasure. Fiji's sex industry is a thriving business.

Natalie was beaten and forced to 'marry' an abusive sailor. When he abandoned her, she was forced to 'marry' again. This sailor beat her so frequently that she constantly feared for her life. Eventually, Natalie bore a son, but her husband denied the child was his and abandoned the young mother and baby.

Desperate — and struggling to raise a child — Natalie saw no other choice, no better life available, than the one she had already been forced into. She began working in a sex hotel until she became pregnant again. Alone and trapped, Natalie had nowhere to turn.

FOR THE FIRST TIME IN HER LIFE, NATALIE FOUND SAFETY AND LOVE.

But there is a God. He is merciful. And we have the privilege of being His arms of compassion for the needy and forsaken.

Natalie learned about the Fiji Homes of Hope — a place for girls fleeing the sex industry — from the brothel "house mother." When the 300-pound house mother could not abort Natalie's baby by jumping on her back, she had to get rid of her because it was "bad luck" for a woman in prostitution to get pregnant.

For the first time in her life, Natalie found safety and love. Her needs were met. She could face the future with hope and dignity. When her baby was born, she compassionately allowed a loving Christian couple to adopt the child.

Natalie began to work on her education with hopes of becoming a teacher. Today, she and her little boy, from her first pregnancy, live on our 40-acre Homes of Hope village located deep in Fiji's jungle. It offers women a chance to flee and heal from their lives of abuse. She has finished her schooling and received her pre-school teaching certificate. She works as the manager of the pre-school in the village and teaches three- to five-year-olds. Her son Shalom is attending the primary school on the village with dreams of being a pilot some day.

We are grateful — astonished, really — by the wonderful success of the WIN program, not only in Fiji, but all around the world. We have a WIN program in the United States as well, providing an opportunity for vulnerable women to gain the skills necessary to become purposeful providers for themselves, their families, and their communities.

WIN also provides another beautiful benefit for the innocent children whose mothers flee the sex slave industry: it breaks the cycle — the generational curse of women on the streets, trapped in a life of sexual abuse and servitude, knowing no other alternative. Their precious youngsters are given a chance to succeed at life. They are offered an education. Most importantly, they are growing up off the streets, in our Homes of Hope, and learning from their moms, who have now become good role models!

With the hope of a secure future and purpose for each day, WIN women gain a well-earned sense of accomplishment.

Natalie's life is one example of hundreds of women whose personal nightmares have given way to significant victory through the Women's Investment Network.

Natalie's horror lasted a decade. But her story has a beautiful ending. It has become a story of redemption, of healing, of a new chance at life. She's no longer weighted down by mounds of back-bending junk — the straw, the mud, the dung.

She is standing on bricks, and from her new vantage point she can see for miles.

LINDA SMITH AT THE 2003 WORLD SUMMIT

CHAPTER 6

Slaves Among Us

You probably know a bright young student just like her. A beautiful smile. Eager to learn. The promise of a successful future ahead.

But *Lin* is also something else. She is a victim of prostitution — fooled and forced into sexual slavery by deceitful masters of the trade. Her tragedy began as a new college student.

Lin lived with her parents and younger brother and sister. They were not a wealthy family. School tuition for her and her siblings was a hefty burden, but a priority.

Soon after Lin started college, her mother's small business failed. Her father's meager salary could not cover the family's cost of living. Lin's part-time job did not help much either. Determined to keep her young brother and sister in school, Lin quit college and began searching for a full-time job.

And then a school acquaintance told Lin about an amazing opportunity in Australia! Young women with a good work ethic were in demand for available jobs — the money potential was wonderful, your travel would be paid for in full. And the best part? You could attend school while there.

Lin knew she would miss her family terribly, but she would be doing the best thing for them. How often do opportunities like this come along?

When she arrived in Australia, Lin found out her new job was in prostitution. She was driven directly to her new job and brutally raped, beaten, and locked up. And the only way out was to pay the traffickers her "debt" — an overwhelming $50,000.

Lin's memories are heartbreaking:

"I fought every man they forced on me for 10 days," she recalls. "I was bloody, bruised, and sick to my stomach. I thought if I fought they would realize I couldn't make money for them and would let me go. But they showed me a picture of a girl who had continued to fight. She was cut up beyond recognition. I felt so bad for her, and completely terrified."

"Worse than that, though," Lin continues, "was the next picture they showed me. It was of me without clothes. If my family saw this, I would be disgraced for life. They would never accept me back. I resolved to pay off the debt by pleasing 900 men."

Morning, noon, and night, Lin's traffickers paraded her before clients. If one of the men chose her, they went into a room which locked from the outside. The clients were allowed to do whatever they wanted to Lin. If she didn't please them, her "owner" would return the client's money, add it to Lin's debt, and withhold food for several days.

Lin was finally rescued out of the brothels, but her "freedom" came at a terrible price: she can never return home. "I live in constant fear," Lin said. "I know too much and have helped other girls. I think they would find me and kill me."

As horrifying as Lin's story is, it is not unique. I hear it over and over again. The names are different. The countries are different. But the deception, violence, and cruelty remain the same.

You might expect governments to get involved, to help. But the shocking truth is quite different. Many officials treat these innocent victims as criminals. Once the women are "discovered," rather than receiving the rehabilitation and justice they deserve, they are deported — routinely flown to countries far from their birth. The unsuspecting girls are then picked up at the airport by the very same trafficking groups they've just escaped and are returned to the nightmare of the brothels that enslave them.

And it is happening right under our noses — hiding in plain sight in big cities, with big budgets and big law enforcement agencies. Lin's story is not from a remote Third World country. It is a story of modern-day slavery, a sophisticated, multi-million-dollar industry. It's concealed under legal and tolerated prostitution like you find in Australia and the Netherlands.

Of course, we want to tell ourselves there is no such thing. We convince ourselves that a girl in "that line of work" is there because she wants to be.

But sex trafficking is a very real, very active business around the world. From the impoverished countries of India and South America to the booming metropolises of Australia, Europe, and the United States, the horror of the sex-trafficking industry appears very much the same. Young women are caught in a vicious cycle: deceived, forced into a life of sexual slavery, sold, and used … again and again — and again.

So, what exactly is sex trafficking?

According to the U.S. Trafficking Victims Protection Act (TVPA), sex trafficking occurs when a commercial sex act is induced by force, fraud, or coercion, or in which the person induced to perform such an act has not attained 18 years of age.

An international rule of law is the United Nations' *Protocol to Prevent, Suppress and Punish Trafficking in Persons, especially Women and Children*. It defines trafficking in persons as "the recruitment, transportation, transfer, harboring, or receipt of persons, by means of threat or use of force or other forms of coercion, of abduction, of fraud, of deception, of the abuse of power, or of a position of vulnerability, or of the giving or receiving of payments or benefits to achieve the consent of a person having control over another person, for the purpose of exploitation. Exploitation shall include, at a minimum, the exploitation of the prostitution of others or other forms of sexual exploitation, forced labour or services, slavery or practices similar to slavery, servitude or the removal of organs. And anyone under the age of 18 years of age in any commercial sex act is always considered a trafficking victim."

WE HAVE A HEART FOR RESTORATION, BRINGING HOPE AND PEACE INTO THE YOUNG LIVES DEVASTATED BY THIS CRUELTY.

What I stumbled upon that dark night on Falkland Road is actually big business — booming business. The horror and degradation are as real in Amsterdam and Australia as they are in Bombay. I will never forget the images — the faces of the desperate and dehumanized. They have propelled me to "take on" an industry so much more engulfing than I ever knew … or wanted to believe existed. But Shared Hope International is dedicated to the fight. We are working worldwide to combat sex trafficking. We have a heart for restoration, bringing hope and peace into the young lives devastated by this cruelty. But we also have a passion for reform, taking legal and political action against the raging monster, the commercial sex industry.

Amsterdam is a prime example of a system gone terribly wrong — a culture tolerant of sexual exploitation and consistent in turning a "blind eye" to the horrors of sex trafficking. Especially to young women who don't speak the language and sometimes don't even know what country they are in. With the legalization of prostitution in Amsterdam came a normalization of Dutch men buying sex, and a culture relying on the sex industry for their economy and the resulting jobs in their tourism industry.

It is extremely difficult to get a visa into Holland for most people from Africa, countries of the former Soviet Union, and poor countries in Asia. But I have testimony from woman after woman who have received a visa without delay or question when trafficked there for the purpose of the sex industry. One girl recalled how she and nine other girls from several African countries were deported to Nigeria. A man met them at the airport and gathered their passports. When he returned, their passports were stamped with a Dutch visa, and the girls were boarded on a commercial plane and sent to Amsterdam to be sold again under the cover of the legal brothel system — Amsterdam's top tourist attraction.

Because trafficking involves the integration of traffickers, buyers, and victims from many cultures and countries, Shared Hope International established a global alliance to bring about more cohesive and effective impact on this illegal trade. The War Against Trafficking Alliance, or WATA, is a multilateral entity that coordinates regional and international efforts to combat sex trafficking. Our initial leading partners in the Alliance were The Protection Project of the Johns Hopkins University School of Advanced International Studies, International Justice Mission, and The

Salvation Army U.S.A.

WATA is held together by a common desire for justice and freedom, and a commitment to seeking strategies for intervention and restoration for victims of international trafficking and the sex industry. We are declaring war on trafficking and mobilizing a coalition of committed individuals, organizations, and institutions in defense of those held captive.

WE ARE DECLARING WAR ON TRAFFICKING . . .

WATA focuses primarily on gathering local leaders at events held around the world. These events are designed to educate activists, increase public awareness, and develop local strategies for progress in the war against trafficking.

In January 2003, we held our first World Summit, where representatives from over 114 nations gathered in Washington, D.C., to focus on comprehensive efforts to eradicate sex trafficking. Two of the first brave little girls whom we rescued, Renu and Ganga, accompanied me. Their lives had been restored, and now they were addressing international delegates about the horrors they had survived.

Then-Secretary of State Colin Powell signed the invitations, and over 800 delegates from all around the world participated. This Summit — part of our vision for Shared Hope from the very earliest days — was an incredible opportunity to develop better strategies and coordinate efforts with world leaders to put an end to modern-day slavery and the exploitation of sex trafficking.

The situation indeed looks grim for the victims. But through efforts like WATA, we are taking on the "bad guys" — the gang members, the crooked government officials who look the other way, the sick predators, and the business-as-usual traffickers. We are exposing the filth behind the filth.

If ever I feel tired, discouraged — too small to make a difference in the face of such a giant — I just close my eyes. I breathe deep. I think of Falkland Road.

I smell the disease, the horror, and the pain of being forsaken. I see the faces, innocent youth stolen, eyes pleading, "I'm beyond hope." And I am determined … resolved. We will not slow down in our efforts to rescue and restore one woman, one child, one life at a time. We will continue spreading hope and love and acceptance to those who are in desperate need.

I can still hear Jesus whispering, "Touch her for Me."

CHAPTER 7

Hunting *the* Hunters

By the time you finish reading this page, another woman or child will be "purchased" by a perverted sex tourist in the Netherlands, Japan, Jamaica, the United States, or some dark corner of the world.

And in case you think, just for a fleeting moment, that "sex tourism" couldn't possibly exist, read on. For the sake of these poor women and children — read on.

Little ***Tojeang*** is from Cameroon. She lived under the heavy hand of an uncle who tried to sell her repeatedly into the sex slave industry. One day, Tojeang met someone who promised her a better life in Europe, caring for children as a career — a golden opportunity to escape the horror-filled life in which she currently lived.

"I was so happy," she said. "I love children." (And my heart broke, because I knew what was coming next.)

A woman accompanied little Tojeang on the flight, always holding her papers and visa. When they arrived in Amsterdam, Tojeang's excitement quickly faded. It turned to dread. Tojeang was brought to a man to service, but she cried and refused. Her handlers beat her and brought another man. And then another. And another.

Tojeang was completely at their mercy. She was prey. Used by men for pleasure. Beaten daily and denied food if a client left unhappy. So when this desperate young woman saw an opportunity to flee — she took it. She ran. And found protection through one of our partner ministries in Amsterdam.

TOJEANG WAS COMPLETELY AT THEIR MERCY. SHE WAS PREY.

Predators are everywhere. In beautiful, scenic Fiji, well-known as a tourist destination, its young, exotic women have sadly become a part of its international "underground" appeal as well.

I learned of an American man, 72 years old, living on a yacht. He waits in front of a local restaurant, watching for vulnerable young women. He spots a 14-year-old school girl. He strikes up a conversation.

This girl, young and trusting, has little knowledge of the world. The kind old man showers her with attention. She knows he can't be dangerous.

Within a few days, her wealthy new friend invites her to his yacht.

I met this girl. Her life was forever changed once she stepped foot on that boat. She will never forget what he did to her that day. She never returned to school.

The old man would bring other girls to the yacht for himself and his friends. Some of the young girls would sail away on yachts, never to be seen again. Some would just be used, videoed, photographed, and then returned to the island.

When I first met this girl, now scarred by abuse and heartache, she was known as the old man's "recruiter," visiting the local towns on the islands, scouting younger girls for him. She told me she did not want to recruit for him anymore, but feared the result of disobedience. The wealthy old man knew the local police, and for the right price, he could have his way.

The laws are weak in Fiji, and in most cases of sexual misconduct or crime, it's the girls who are considered to be at fault. There are no laws enforced to penalize those who would commercially exploit a child.

This young "recruiter" told me how she had brought one girl out to the yacht, watched as she was given to a man on a nearby boat — then later saw the girl floating face down in the water.

"I don't want to die," she told me.

One of the young women at our Homes of Hope in Fiji arranged for me to meet girls she knew who had been forced into prostitution. The girl I just described was one of them. That discussion made it clear to me that most of the girls had been photographed in the nude and with sex acts video-taped. People log on every day to watch streaming video of children being raped. Every day, thousands of predators find their victims online and travel thousands of miles to exploit them.

And then there's the precious six-year-old boy from South Africa. This helpless child was snatched from his home, ravaged and tortured by human predators. If you can call them human.

The boy's pimp handed the young child over to two airline stewards who tied him up with barbed wire, raped him, and violated him using a small pineapple.

The attack was so cruel the pimp couldn't even stand to watch. He went into the restroom and smoked crack to get high. But even the drugs couldn't drown out the child's cries and frantic pleas for help.

I know you feel disgusted. I know you want to throw this book in the trash and try to forget what you just read. But that sick feeling in the pit of your stomach — that stinging behind your eyes — reveals your compassion. That heated flush across your face is anger.

I know. I feel it, too.

I have never felt such rage. How can anyone be so heartless, so sadistic and cruel? They are nothing more than perverted predators.

And they are stalking children. It doesn't matter the city — Cape Town, South Africa; the island of Fiji; Kingston, Jamaica; Amsterdam, Netherlands; Las Vegas, Nevada — places where commercial sex has become a thriving, lucrative business.

EVERY DAY, THOUSANDS OF PREDATORS FIND THEIR VICTIMS ONLINE AND TRAVEL THOUSANDS OF MILES TO EXPLOIT THEM.

We must stop them. The hunters must become the hunted.

The stories that just made you feel sick are what many consider "entertainment." The commercial sex industry, which includes both prostitution and pornography, is now a multi-billion-dollar industry.

Shared Hope International undertook a 12-month review of the demand and operation of sex tourism in four major markets: the United States, the Netherlands, Japan, and Jamaica. Our project was funded by the U.S. Department of State's Trafficking in Persons Office.

Our discoveries were chilling — but not surprising. The report revealed that in each locale, there was exploding, visible growth in the tolerance and acceptance of the commercial sex market. This in turn, promoted the "invisible" growth of the sex trafficking market, supplying persons for sexual exploitation to meet the booming demand.

Think of Tojeang. Think of that innocent

six-year-old boy. They are viewed and used as human commodities. *Product.*

And we are culpable. Cultural tolerance — in other words, you and I pretending that trafficking doesn't exist — forms the backdrop for the operation of commercial sex markets and dictates their breadth, diversity, and strength. The demand generated by each of these markets then dictates the extent of the trafficking in persons required to meet the overwhelming need for human product.

THOSE WHO BUY COMMERCIAL SEX ARE DEMANDING TO HAVE SEX WITH YOUNGER AND YOUNGER VICTIMS.

Equally disturbing was our finding that younger and younger females are being recruited and exploited in commercial sex markets in all locations. Those who buy commercial sex are demanding to have sex with younger and younger victims.

As I learned more about the exploding sex-trafficking industry, it was obvious that we couldn't stop with our Homes of Hope and the WIN program. It was clear we would have to give equal energy — perhaps even greater energy — to the "prevention" prong of our three-pronged prevention-rescue-restoration strategy. The horrors I had witnessed firsthand compelled me: I would have to do everything within my power to end this modern-day slavery.

And so, we extended our reach once again and took on the Predator Project.

Through the giving and support of friends of Shared Hope International, we are committed to doing everything in our power to stop those who hurt women and children and to offer hope and love to those rescued.

SHARED HOPE INTERNATIONAL

Restoring life to the hopeless

☐ **Yes, Linda,** I want to be a part of the incredible efforts of Shared Hope International to not only restore sex slaves, but also to stop those who create the demand and those who provide women and children as the "products" in the commercial sex industry.
I enclose: $_____

For timely updates on our efforts, please send your email address:

_____

To send your gift via debit or credit card, fill in the information below:

☐ **Visa**   ☐ **MasterCard**   ☐ **Discover**

Card No. _____ **Exp.** _____
Gift Amount _____
Name _____
Signature _____
Address: _____
City: _____ **State:** _____ **ZIP:** _____

Thank you for your love and generosity. All gifts are tax deductible as allowed by law. Please make checks payable to Shared Hope International and return to Shared Hope International, P.O. Box 65337, Vancouver, WA 98665. Gifts received exceeding those needed to meet immediate requirements will be used to help other women and children through Shared Hope's vital work around the world.

This project takes drastic measures to stop traffickers — anyone who sells women and children for money — and their sick customers.

We began launching investigations to uncover sexual predators and expose marketplaces of victimization around the world.

Our Predator Project focuses on profiling and punishing those who prey on and profit from exploiting vulnerable women and children. This effort collaborates with local law enforcement, government officials, and the public by disclosure of information.

Our strategy involves exposing the perpetrators who facilitate the sex-trafficking markets and those who create the demand for these victims by following a "three Ps" approach:

Prevention: developing public awareness campaigns to help educate the public and raise awareness of sex trafficking, especially as it relates to demand, such as Shared Hope's "The Defenders USA." This effort equips men to say NO to buying commercial sex through prostitution and pornography.

Prosecution: researching and gathering information for law enforcement about how predators work in order to dismantle trafficking operations around the world, Shared Hope has been successful in this effort through the Predator Project.

Protection: partnering with local non-government organizations and boosting their capacity to assist victims of sex trafficking, Shared Hope has accomplished this through our Homes of Hope program, which includes the Women's Investment Network and the War Against Trafficking Alliance.

I am determined that the monsters who populate the global sex trafficking industry will pay a much higher price than they expect to destroy the life of a child.

Our goal is that the Predator Project will expose those who victimize women and children and prosecute brothel owners and traffickers who make their money by inflicting life-long pain.

Maybe it seems I've gone overboard. But it doesn't feel overboard to me. As you read these stories, I am seeing their faces. Little girls trapped in a life of horror and fear, viciously and savagely hunted like animals of prey. These precious children are real. But they are not living a life beyond hope. There is a God. And He will embrace them — if we will be His arms of compassion ... His hands of mercy.

Do you feel sick? Do your eyes sting with tears? Is your face flushed in anger? Then reach. Touch. Rescue. Restore. One woman — one child — one at a time.

CHAPTER 8

In the Backyard

A young girl stood on the corner just outside of town. Her clothes drew judgmental glares from passersby because they revealed her occupation. She was a prostitute.

Some looked at her with contempt. Others looked at her as less than human, useful only to satisfy their sexual cravings.

A middle-aged widower and father of three approached her. She knew him well. He was a wealthy landowner from a prominent family well known for their shrewd dealings in business.

But he didn't know her. To him she was just a prostitute, and his only hesitation was that he had no cash on him at the moment.

The price he promised was good, but the woman insisted on a deposit. His ring, bracelet, and walking stick would do.

The terms now determined, this young woman went with the man — old enough to be her father. He never asked her name or where she was from. He never asked about her family, faith, or interests. Instead, he entered into the mystery of human sexuality — that intimate act intended by God to unite a man and woman in an everlasting bond — without even knowing she was *the widow of his own son.*

. . . SHE WAS THE WIDOW OF HIS OWN SON.

Men almost never ask about the woman they buy for sex. Why should they? She is just a prostitute, and the label "prostitute" allows men and society to treat her as a slave or less than human. The culture of tolerance that allows men to buy sex provides a convenient label that creates a mental disconnect. This is not a little girl who is someone's daughter, sister, or niece. She is just a prostitute.

Not much has changed in this regard for girls in more than 4,000 years, when the story of the businessman and the widow actually took place. This is the story of Judah and Tamar, told in the biblical book of Genesis.

Tamar reminds me of someone I met through my work. Charity was 12 years old when her stepfather first abused her. Tamar was most likely a young child as well.

Charity's stepfather gave her no value. He stole her worth and discarded her.

Tragedy had struck Tamar too. Judah's son died shortly after they married. In those days, a woman was seen as worthless unless she was married. That's why the law provided for the woman by requiring an unmarried brother-in-law or nearest relative to marry her if she became widowed.

So Tamar married Judah's second son. But he died also. The law required Judah to give her to his third son:

"Judah then said to his daughter-in-law Tamar, 'Live as a widow in your father's house until my son Shelah grows up.' For he thought, 'He may die too, just like his brothers.' So Tamar went to live in her father's house" (Gen. 38:11).

Imagine this little girl, yanked from her childhood to become a woman and wife, only to see two husbands die and then to have her father-in-law reject her and send her away. Without a husband or a son, Tamar had no future. Who else would have her? She was already used and getting older.

Now imagine Charity. An all-American girl yanked from her childhood by an abusive stepfather. What future could Charity have now that he had stolen her value in her eyes and rejected her worth? So Charity fled. She fled to the streets and the unknown rather than suffer from the monster in her home.

American runaways are typically on the streets for less than 48 hours before a pimp preys on them, according to The National Incidence Studies of Missing, Abducted, Runaway, and Throwaway Children.

Charity met a truck driver who was very kind. He offered her a warm truck to stay in and filled her mind with flattering words. She didn't mind so much when he began to abuse her. After all, he wasn't mean like her stepfather. She didn't understand exactly what he was doing when he sold her to other truck drivers or when he eventually sold her to another pimp with whom she would stay. All she knew for sure was that she was surviving.

Tamar was doing the same thing — surviving — when she put the harlot's veil over her face.

. . . WE MUST LOOK BEYOND THE VEIL.

"When Tamar was told, 'Your father-in-law is on his way to Timnah to shear his sheep,'" Genesis 38:13,14 says, "she took off her widow's clothes, covered herself with a veil to disguise herself, and then sat down at the entrance to Enaim, which is on the road to Timnah. For she saw that, though Shelah had now grown up, she had not been given to him as his wife."

Judah never saw Tamar because of the veil, which in that culture was the sign of a harlot. To him she was a faceless body. The men who bought Charity never saw her real face either. She wore an emotional veil, like every prostituted woman. She must smile so he thinks she enjoys his masculine advances. She has to flirt and seduce to bring the required quota back to her enslaver. If she fails, her pimp will beat and starve her and make her believe it's her fault. She believes she has let him down and deserves to be punished.

SHE NEEDS A DEFENDER — AN INSTINCT GOD PLACED IN MAN.

There is another side to this emotional veil: the prostituted girls must also be tough. She must claim that the life she is living is her choice. The pain she feels must never be exposed. When people try to help her, she often behaves rudely and seems mean. And she would never dream of being a "bad girl" by snitching on her pimp. She wants approval more than anything.

If we are to discover who these little girls are, we must look beyond the veil. We must ask this child where she came from, to learn that she is someone's daughter.

She is just a little girl. But society labels these girls "prostitutes." Even the men who buy sex feel no guilt when they call her "ho" or "slut." "She's just a bad girl," they think. "She doesn't deserve to be treated like a human." It does not occur to them that this is a child in need of rescue and justice. She needs a defender — an instinct God placed in man.

Judah did not defend Tamar. He used her because he thought she was a prostitute and therefore deserved to be used. But when he heard rumors that his daughter-in-law had prostituted herself and was pregnant, he became enraged and ordered her execution. He somehow thought he was guiltless for having bought sex — yet he wanted Tamar burned for selling sex.

There is never any good in either buying or selling sex. In Charity's case, pimps forced, coerced, and manipulated her to sell her body. She was a victim. Men thought they had a right to her body because she was called a prostitute, but this is a form of modern-day slavery. The 2006 Trafficking Victims Protection Act calls her a victim of a violent crime.

When the Pharisees brought Jesus a woman caught in adultery, He agreed that the law condemned the sin. So He ordered, "If any one of you is without sin, let him be the first to throw a stone at her."

The accusing Pharisees all dropped their stones and went home. Jesus set the adulteress free, saying, "Go now and leave your life of sin."

The truth will ultimately come out. These precious children, victims of abuse, can be restored. And they deserve to be rescued. Charity is now a woman. She clings to the freedom Christ gave her, and in turn she gives her life to serving women and girls rescued out of prostitution. She serves them day and night, proving that though the world treats these girls as if they have no value, God sees them differently — as precious gifts.

Our girls need us to help them. Society has rejected them because of the label "prostitute." How can a girl flee her pimp if society rejects her?

Shared Hope International partners with good people throughout the United States and the world who accept these girls as they are. These outreaches offer hope and restoration. These are places where a girl can once again stand with dignity and her God-given value.

Tamar grew beyond her family betrayal as well. In fact, the very family that at first rejected her later held her in the highest honor. "She is more righteous than I," Judah said (Genesis 38:26).

Her name was included in a blessing given at an engagement announcement for Jewish men: "May you have standing in Ephrathah and be famous in Bethlehem. Through the offspring the Lord gives you by this young woman, may your family be like that of Perez, whom Tamar bore to Judah" (Ruth 4:11-12).

Yet Tamar's ultimate redemption didn't change the awful truth about women being used as commercial objects. And just as the truth came out with Tamar, Charity's story opened the door to reveal a dark secret — an escalating pattern of sexual exploitation and forced prostitution in the United States.

"Data reveals at least 100,000 kids and as many as 293,000 children have become commodities [in the sex industry] and most of America has missed it," said Ernie Allen, President and Chief Executive Officer of the National Center for Missing and Exploited Children.

Each day brings a new story of yet another arrest and more traumatized victims. My heart is broken by each story of deception, violence, and the hideous robbing of innocence.

And the pain grows greater as we realize the awful truth — these American girls are being used primarily by American men. American men, our neighbors and friends, using 14-year-olds — children who may have grown up in your neighborhood, gone to your child's school, or played with your kids.

One of the largest crackdowns on child prostitution rings in the United States exposed operations in Florida, Michigan, New Jersey, Pennsylvania, and Ohio. In a coordinated effort by the U.S. Justice Department, the FBI's Criminal Investigative Division, and the National Center for Missing and Exploited Children (NCMEC), authorities identified and rescued more than 30 child victims and arrested 31 adults, charging them in the sex trafficking of children.

"This is a crime of hidden victims," said John Rabun, Vice President of NCMEC. "Many think child trafficking is only a problem in foreign countries, but nothing can be further from the truth."

Rebecca grew up in Kingston, Arizona. She enjoyed school and earned good grades. But life at home was unstable, and Rebecca's life began to deteriorate.

She began using methamphetamines when she was only 13 years old. Her own mom was the first to offer the drugs to her. Rebecca lived without a father and with abuse, neglect, and financial struggles. Her mother returned to jail often. Rebecca moved in and out of different homes.

At 14, she became trapped in the dark manipulation of sexual exploitation. She ran away from home and wound up hopeless and helpless on the streets.

A man approached her and sold her a dream. He promised Rebecca a good life, a nice home, and more money than she could ever imagine.

The good life he promised her actually involved servicing men — the more men, the more money (of which she kept none). The job description included beatings and bruises, rape, and brutalities beyond description.

When asked why she stayed — why she never ran — her answer is simple. "That life," she said, "was all I knew."

This is not a story of India. This is not Fiji. This is not the red light district in Amsterdam where prostitution is legal. This is our beloved homeland. And Rebecca is one of thousands trapped here in America in a horrible life with no hope of anything better. Little American girls — sold a dream of something better — and fooled into a life of modern-day slavery.

One of the biggest offenders, by far, is the city of Las Vegas. Here, sex trafficking flourishes. I went to Vegas. This was not a holiday. It was an investigative expedition, like my first trip to India — I had to see for myself. Even after so many years of working with women and girls victimized by the sex industry, what I saw stunned me.

The sex tourism industry is in plain view in Las Vegas, a place where prostitution is illegal, but thriving.

In parts of Nevada, prostitution is legal, but in Las Vegas, it is simply tolerated and even facilitated. Some claim that legalization enables authorities to control the industry and keep it safe. My research and experience reveals legalized and tolerated prostitution actually increases demand. I saw the ugly truth firsthand.

At four o'clock in the morning, some of the gambling windows are closed down on the main floor of a large and popular casino, but this is when the buying and selling of young girls begins in earnest. I saw girls draped over the shoulders of middle-aged men still playing the tables, men old enough to be their grandfathers.

I watched as the concierge arranged a "deal" between a customer and a girl. Security officers just looked the other way.

How did these girls get here? I'll tell you because I know. I have heard their painful stories time and time again. Some have been abducted. Some have been lured. Only a few have been trafficked in from outside the country. They are all lost and confused. They have no idea how far they are from home — or if they will ever see home again. Some are runaways from abusive homes, desperate and alone; they trusted the wrong grown-up and landed in a situation far beyond their control. They have been violated, tortured, gang-raped, and destroyed in mind, body, and spirit. They have been moved to Las Vegas — or some other American city — and put to work. One day a child, the next day a slave.

As I walked the streets in the middle of the night, dozens of hawkers handed out business cards to men passing by. Many cards showed pictures of sex acts too crude to describe. Each advertised a phone number to call.

Free newspaper-style vending machines line Vegas's famous "Strip." But they do not contain newspapers. They contain expensive-looking magazines, all offering page after page of enticing photos and the same phone numbers as the hawkers' business cards.

Vegas is a hub for traffickers in the United States.

HUMAN TRAFFICKING IS FACILITATED BY ACCEPTANCE.

To think of these very young girls, trapped and hopeless, being led to a hotel room by a man in the middle of the night is unbearable. Young girls should be protected, not exploited.

If someone told Americans that there are 5,000 slaves being harbored in some American city, wouldn't they be up in arms? Wouldn't they storm the streets and demand justice?

Yet slave traders snatch little girls from communities all over the United States and force them into a life of sexual slavery in Las Vegas — and all is quiet. Where are the protests?

Human trafficking is facilitated by acceptance. We think of these girls as "wanting it" — we turn our heads in disgust at the girls who seemingly chose this life. "Slaves in the United States?" No such thing, we say.

But these girls are victims. Cruel people manipulate, coerce, and physically force them into a nightmare. The girls succumb to the pimp out of fear and desperation. Someone else chose this life for most of these girls when they were 12 or 13 years old. They did not choose this life. Tragically, once a girl is used as a sexual product, society labels her "prostitute." This is wrong. Her label should read: RAPED, TORTURED, ENSLAVED. Prostitution is a brutal, violent industry. The young girl is most often the one criminalized, while the sick buyer (the "john") and the vicious seller (the "pimp") are rarely even mentioned.

In one Las Vegas court room, charges were brought against 183 youth picked up for prostitution in a 14-month period ending December 2006. In the same time frame, there were only two instances where the buyers and sellers of children in the thriving Las Vegas sex industry were arrested .

While children are the ones criminalized, their abusers are rarely arrested or charged with a crime. What injustice!

At Shared Hope, we are pushing for laws to be written, strengthened, and enforced to change this. We are working to expose the truth behind America's heart-rending "dark secret." Yes, sex trafficking is rampant around the world. But God forbid we should attack the problem in every nation on earth and allow our own children, here in North America, to be taken, used, and destroyed by predators.

Yes, we have our work cut out for us. While our efforts on behalf of victimized women and children around the world must never falter, we are determined to devote ourselves to the overwhelming, life-shattering sex trafficking industry steadily growing here at home — right in our own backyard.

CHAPTER 9

Rescue Upstream

Over time, I've come to think of our work in terms of a kind of fable.

A man and his family are out in the country. They're enjoying a picnic on a beautiful summer day, in a clearing with a lovely river flowing nearby. Just like my own husband, who loves to play baseball with our children, this man is playing the all-American sport with his children and their friends.

After several games, however, his stamina just can't match that of the younger kids. He begs them to stop for a bit. "A little rest and we'll start again," he promises, to their protests. Exhausted, he collapses to the ground.

But not for long. In the moment of quiet, he hears

a faint cry for help. Glancing quickly around at his own children, he realizes they're all safe. He looks to the river. In horror, he sees a head bobbing out in the rough current. A child. Without a thought but for that one struggling child, the man races to the river and jumps in.

Already exhausted from the baseball game, the man isn't sure he can wrestle the current and rescue the child. But he fights with all of his might and brings the child to shore. Suddenly, he realizes just how close his own kids are to real danger. The river that once seemed so beautiful, such a natural part of the landscape, is actually a rushing, raging trap.

As he sits down to catch his breath, still shaking from the horrible scare, he hears another sound. Turning his head back toward the river, he sees another child. Again, without hesitation, the man jumps to his feet and runs to the river's edge. He plunges into the torrent and rescues the child, dragging her to the bank.

But one after another, over and over again, come the desperate cries for help. Other picnicking families now join him in the valiant rescue attempts — swimming as quickly as they can to rescue one child at a time.

Rescue teams and fire trucks arrive. Out jumps the fire chief — a big guy. He takes one look at the situation and begins to run the wrong way. The exhausted people, aching from their heroic work, cry out: "Wrong way! We need help! There are still so many children!"

He answers without delay. "I know. I have to go upstream."

He realizes that somehow, for some reason, the children keep falling into the river somewhere upstream. A riverbank has collapsed, perhaps, or a fence has been broken through. More and more children will plunge into the deadly river unless someone fixes the source of the problem.

And we, too, must hurry upstream.

We have been pulling girls out of the river. The work is exhausting. So often we get worn out. We are fighting so valiantly down stream, swimming with all of our strength, bringing one precious, vulnerable life to the shore at a time. It is valuable, crucial work. And we will not quit.

MORE AND MORE CHILDREN WILL PLUNGE INTO THE DEADLY RIVER UNLESS SOMEONE FIXES THE SOURCE OF THE PROBLEM.

But with each victim we pull from the raging river, the torrent of the commercial sex industry, we hear the desperate cries of more.

Someone, somewhere — some monster — is creating a demand for these girls we're rescuing ... these girls we have come to love so completely. My life has been dedicated to building safe places for them and their babies, helping them re-build their lives after the traumatic, near-death experience of being swept away by the engulfing currents of prostitution and pornography — the industry's raging river.

Now — out of that same love and concern — we must also work to keep them from falling in.

Yes, at times I feel overwhelmed. Sometimes I feel burdened with the girls' numerous problems. Sometimes I grow weary with the financial struggle of just keeping the lights on, food on the table, and medical needs covered. Sometimes, I don't think I can do one more thing. Fighting the bad guys who buy and sell these girls, it seems, requires more energy than I have.

But then I think of Ganga. I think of Renu, of Shoba, of Pooja. I think of all my precious girls and the nightmares they survived. They kept fighting. And so will I.

Not long ago, Shared Hope International was asked to do a review and write a report on the commercial exploitation of children in America. Each country does its own analysis for submission to the World Congress every four years.

At first, I thought this would be easy — compared to "backward" countries we have researched such as India, Indonesia, Nepal, Singapore, Argentina, and South Africa. But what I discovered as I made my way upstream was astonishingly terrible: the United States is really no different. The river is raging, swirling, threatening — and our own kids are helplessly falling in.

We must start building fences and barriers. We must start putting up warning signs. The shore is crumbling into the river, eroding with time. It gives the appearance of a stable edge, but it is just a thin veneer of safety, covering a deep and swirling current of danger.

The sex industry is out to destroy your children. They want to recruit your son online as a potential buyer. They need your 13-year-old daughter as product. And they won't stop there. They want your husband, brother, and friend.

In today's society, thousands of regular, everyday guys are using and abusing children for purposes of sexual perversion.

And one of the leading causes of this overwhelming demand for sex is Internet pornography. The images feed the market. They distort and desensitize — replayed in your mind again and again until it just doesn't seem "so bad." In fact, more than 32 million individuals visit an online porn site every month. And of all porn sites, one out of every five pornographic images is of a child. A child just like so many we each know — starved for attention and totally unaware of the evils of this world.

The market is active and overwhelming. There is a broad spectrum of temptation, from the young boy's first brush with Internet pornography to the man in prison for sexual assault (over 70% of incarcerated sex offenders admit to fueling their addiction by viewing child pornography) — every guy is a target. And every guy has the potential to fall.

Randy will tell you it's just like falling off a cliff, out of control, spinning 100 miles an hour toward the ground.

I TRULY BELIEVE IT IS GOING TO TAKE MEN TO STOP MEN.

In the beginning, Randy was obsessed with the game of basketball. His life revolved around it. It was his only passion, until — at the age of 45 — Randy hit rock bottom after the death of one of his children. He couldn't sleep. He became depressed. That's when he became heavily involved in Internet pornography. It was a means of escape — his new passion. Once again, Randy was riding high at the top of his game — with his porn addiction.

But the subjects of Randy's attention online were eventually too young; and one afternoon, federal agents walked into his office and exposed his secret life. Randy spent two years in prison. Still, he says today he had never felt freer — he was finally living in the light of truth, no longer in the dark shadows of obsession and addiction.

We ran our own Shared Hope study and found most men first get involved in pornography between the ages of 11 and 15. A surprising 54% admitted they considered themselves "addicted to pornography" at some point in their life; 19.4% said they were presently addicted. An overwhelming 82% said the Internet had changed their consumption of pornography, making it more readily available. Let's call it what it is: sexual abuse at the click of a mouse. Most don't think of it that way. But I have countless stories of violated little girls who will prove to you otherwise.

As I surveyed the damage the commercial sex industry has wreaked on our nation's children, now compiled in a report called the *U.S. Mid-Term Review on Commercial Sexual Exploitation of Children in America,* I was convinced that it was time to enlist more concerned men in the war on sex enslavement. I truly believe it is going to take men to stop men.

So we created "The Defenders USA."

The Defenders USA are men invested in America's children and determined to protect their futures from predators in the commercial sex industry. They have joined together to take a strong stand, declaring that the sexual exploitation of children, use of pornography, and buying sex is not something real men will tolerate.

Yes, we are "working against the tide" — struggling upstream, so to speak. In fact, when we showed a public service announcement created by The Defenders USA to the U.S. State Department, one of the staffers exclaimed just that: "You're working upstream!"

And the more I thought about her words, the more convinced I became that we are working in the right direction.

Take **Brianne**. She was 16. Came from a difficult home life.

They met for the first time in a restaurant. He befriended her over time and eventually asked to take her to a "babysitting job."

When she arrived, she was pistol-whipped, forced to have sex, and then held in a closet for months. Eventually she was sold for sex — then sold again, and again, over and over — until finally, mercifully, she was rescued.

In Baltimore, **Monique** was placed in the care of her uncle. To feed his drug habit, he turned her into a sex slave for hire.

Brianne. Monique. Prostitutes — or slaves?

The sad, true stories could go on and on, each more sickening than the last. And each story would punctuate the fact that these children are not "child prostitutes." They are victims. Slaves. Manipulated and abused. Their innocence has been savagely stolen — not by wild-eyed, creepy-looking creatures, but rather, in many cases, by ordinary, everyday guys — uncles, fathers, co-workers, and neighbors. All just seeking some new sexual thrill because over time, a steady stream of pornography has twisted their minds.

GANGA AND KANHAIYA

CHAPTER 10

Full Circle

That moment long ago, when I innocently took that life-changing phone call in my D.C. office, I would never have imagined this course for my life. But my phone rang, I picked it up, and I found myself suddenly heading down a very different path.

Yes, it was difficult. I endured my days of doubt and confusion — wondering why I was there, praying desperately that God would send someone else. As I set foot in that first brothel, humanity overwhelmed me, and I rejected that tiny human casualty of a raging, monstrous industry. It shames me now — I couldn't stand the way she smelled. But God had something else in mind — "Touch her for Me," He whispered — and continues to whisper — in my ear.

Strangely, I don't smell it anymore. I don't find it

repulsive. God healed me in a dynamic way. The smell now means something different to me ... it means dung in the bricks. It means broken girls getting it together, getting stronger. It means hope.

In all the darkness of this work, any one girl would be worth every effort, every tear shed, every dollar given. Ganga alone would have been worth it all. She was one of my first girls. Today, this wonderful young woman of India is like a daughter to my husband and me. Shared Hope provided her first home after her flight from a life of terrible abuse and helped to restore her hope and joy.

Ganga now manages daily training at the Homes of Hope Village in Bombay. She works with the girls and children who have just come out of the brothels. She understands completely how they have suffered.

When I visit India, I love to see Ganga. A recent trip was no different. I should have known something was up, though, as I walked into the circle of women's homes at the Village. Instead of wearing her typical bib overalls, when I arrived I found Ganga dressed in a lovely sari and beaming with a huge smile. She was so radiant that for a moment, I almost didn't recognize her.

GANGA ALONE WOULD HAVE BEEN WORTH IT ALL.

Ganga had met the love of her life!

This lovely, once hopeless, once utterly destroyed young woman has now married a wonderful young man. Kanhaiya, her husband, was taken off the streets 10 years ago by our partner ministry, Bombay Teen Challenge, as a supposedly hopeless drug addict. Today, he has been restored — trained as an electrician — and he ministers to other addicts by training them ... giving them "purpose for the day."

Ganga has come full circle. Just telling her story, I can't help but smile as only a proud mother would.

GANGA HAS COME FULL CIRCLE.

Ganga's life testifies to the fact that there is hope. The problems we confront every day are serious — agonizingly serious — but they are not cause for unremitting despair. I have found my own journey to be a journey of hope, of healing, of joy, of restoration. Today, I am able to stand on my anger, my disgust and sorrow — and it raises me up. My rage against the predators pushes me. Righteous indignation proves to be a mighty force for accomplishing good work. One might even call it God's work.

I am not asking you to travel to India and walk down Falkland Road. I am not telling you to go to Amsterdam and try to stop the traffickers. I am not expecting you to head to Capitol Hill and plead this cause.

But today, you can open your eyes to the reality of this nightmare. You can change your language — never label a girl a "prostitute" again. She is, in reality, being prostituted. She is a victim. She is a slave. You can join The Defenders USA by visiting our website: www.thedefendersusa.org. Invite others to do the same.

You can support Shared Hope International in our efforts to eradicate sexual slavery from the world stage. I know it seems like a huge undertaking, but it is my calling, and I will keep battling as long as God gives me the ability. My determination is renewed with every little face I see filled with hurt and hopelessness. I want to shout, "Look at Ganga! There is hope! There is real hope!"

We are working to train prosecutors and judges about the reality of this industry. We are working to see tough laws passed against trafficking and forced prostitution. We are headed upstream; we are pouring poison on the roots; we are building fences to protect our children.

We have hope. We have the living evidence of our beautiful Ganga and all of our rescued girls. We have stories of redemption and programs of restoration. It has been nearly a decade of incredible brick-making, long hours of gathering straw and mixing mud. But we are determined to keep on building. And you can join in.

All you have to do is show up.

ABOUT SHARED HOPE:

Our Mission

Shared Hope International exists to prevent sex trafficking, restore its victims, and bring justice to women and children affected by this devastating crime. We envision a world passionately opposed to sex trafficking and a committed community restoring survivors to lives of purpose, value, and choice — one life at a time. We strive to create a world where every survivor is surrounded by trained professionals, an alert community, just law and policy, knowledgeable service providers, and appropriate shelter options.

Our Values

As Christian abolitionists, we believe survivors of sex trafficking deserve the opportunity to be restored to dignity and purpose, regardless of their faith or system of belief. As Christian stewards, we prayerfully seek to use wisdom and biblical guidance for every dollar we spend. As Christian leaders, we seek to inspire change by informing and empowering activists, providing strategic guidance to local shelter and service partners, and influencing policy-makers and first responders.

Our Programs

Prevent

Training — Our training programs and resources equip professionals and community members to advance the network of protection offered to trafficking survivors and potential victims.

Research — Through research we promote the creation of promising practices and the development of effective intervention and response.

Awareness — We initiate campaigns that raise alarm in communities and provide education to teens and parents on the warning signs of trafficking.

The Defenders USA — A coalition of men who take a pledge opposing all forms of commercialized sex. Defenders educate, equip, and empower men to fight against the demand side of domestic minor sex trafficking.

Collaboration — We share our expertise and resources with task forces, law enforcement agencies, community groups, and others to accelerate solutions to combat trafficking.

Restore

Local Partnerships — By providing funding and technical assistance to programs operated by local partners internationally and in the U.S., we offer safe homes, medical care, education, vocational training, therapy, and outreach and intervention services for survivors.

Women's Investment Network (WIN) — Helps women gain practical job experience and is a component of all Shared Hope partner programs.

Terry's House — An independent living home operated by Shared Hope for young women over 18. The home offers residents an affordable housing option while they pursue education or vocational training.

National Restoration Initiative — Shared Hope launched this initiative to build upon the lessons and good practices of current shelter and service providers. Through this initiative we conduct research, host national forums, and partner with local shelter and service organizations.

Bring Justice

We help strengthen trafficking laws and build better policies to protect victims by providing comprehensive legal research, expert testimony, coalition support, and advocacy initiatives. Justice initiatives include:

The Protected Innocence Challenge — An annual Report Card on the sufficiency of child sex-trafficking laws in each state and recommendations for improvement.

The Demanding Justice Project — A research and advocacy initiative to increase attention and advocacy for anti-demand efforts.

JuST Response — Brings together our research on services for domestic minor sex-trafficking victims with our analysis of state statutory protective responses. By merging research on implementation efforts and policy analysis, the JuST Response seeks to stimulate well informed legislative efforts that lead to improved protective responses.

SHARED HOPE RESOURCES

FILMS

The *Chosen* film series teaches teens the warning signs of trafficking through the true stories of teenage girls who were tricked by traffickers. Learn how pimps and gangs are luring youth into the commercial sex industry and how teens can protect themselves and others. The resource packages include additional educational tools to further discussion, learning, and action!

Chosen. Two "All-American" teenage girls who were tricked by traffickers recount how the unthinkable happened to them. Brianna, 18, was a star student, cheerleader, and waitress. Lacy, 13, enjoyed church and volunteering in her community. Both were skillfully targeted by traffickers and manipulated into the dangerous commercial sex market. (Run Time: 21:34)

Chosen — Gang Edition. Lured by promises of love and protection, Maria was recruited by a gang at 12 years old. For five years, she was forced to sacrifice her body to Mexican drug runs, prostitution, and violence. Trapped in a world she never expected, she was forced to make the ultimate decision: surrender her life to the gang or risk escape. (Run Time: 12:48)

Chosen PLUS – (Available in English and Spanish) *Chosen PLUS –* is the most comprehensive youth sex trafficking prevention film and resource package available! Package includes both *Chosen* and *Chosen — Gang Edition* films and accompanying resources.

BOOKS

From Congress to the Brothel: A Journey of Hope, Healing, and Restoration by Linda Smith. Walk with Linda as she relives her life-altering journey that began in one of the worst brothel districts in India. Hear her extraordinary encounter with child sex slavery around the globe.

Renting Lacy: A Story of America's Prostituted Children by Linda Smith. Based on actual encounters, Linda exposes the underworld of child sex trafficking in America by telling the stories of those who live there, the traffickers, the buyers, and the victims who struggle to survive each night.

RESEARCH

We believe effective response is informed response. Shared Hope heavily invests in providing policy leaders, community advocates, and first responders with data-driven, comprehensive studies to create better solutions to fight trafficking.

TRAINING

Gang TRAP Training Guide and Video Series. This unique training tool addresses the growing trend of sex trafficking by criminal street gangs. The guide targets law enforcement, service providers, and prosecutors, offering instruction on gang trafficking dynamics, recruitment and control tactics, common professional challenges with these cases, therapeutic response, and collaboration. The accompanying 60-minute video addresses the same topics through interviews with experts and survivors.

Domestic Minor Sex Trafficking: Identifying and Responding to America's Trafficked Youth Training Guide and Video Series. This interactive training tool offers a comprehensive guide to domestic minor sex trafficking including the law, victim vulnerabilities, trafficker tactics, and effective responses for agencies and organizations. The 40-minute video allows viewers to hear from experts and survivors, watch pimps engage with buyers, and discover the reality of child sex trafficking.

Intervene: Identifying and Responding to America's Prostituted Youth. Intervene is designed for service providers and clinicians to improve identification and response to victims of sex trafficking. The Practitioner Guide addresses vulnerability factors of potential victims, common trafficker tactics, and the impact of trauma on survivors. The Intake Tool is a tiered set of questions to identify exploited youth while reducing the risk of re-traumatization. This package includes two training videos, *Intervene* and *Gang TRAP*.

Please visit SharedHope.org/Resources to find information on prices, fact sheets, and many other useful materials.

TESTIMONIES

My name is Manisha Sunuwar. I am 20 years old. Asha Nepal has been my home since I was 7.

I knew nothing about myself — I didn't know where I came from, who my parents were, where my home was, nothing. I learned the bitter truth from another resident at Asha Nepal: Renu, whom I call my "Aunty."

Born in a small village in central Nepal, my mother grew up very poor. At 16, she fell in love with a man who offered her a job and a better life in the city. But she was betrayed and sold in India. She soon got pregnant with me, but she did not want a baby: a boy was destined to be a criminal, a girl a sex slave like her. She wanted to get rid of me, so she started neglecting me.

That's when my dear Aunty Renu, also trafficked to the same brothel, began caring for me, while encouraging my mother to send me to someplace I could be saved. But both of them were helpless until the wonderful day my Aunty was rescued — by Bombay Teen Challenge. She urged my mother to take me, to seek shelter there, but my mother was not convinced. Instead, she sent me to a relative in Nepal while she stayed to work. I am told that I lived there for three years.

Eventually, my Aunty Renu came to Nepal and searched for me. When she found me she saw that I was miserable and was being used by these relatives as anything for money. She immediately arranged to bring me to Asha Nepal. Asha Nepal gave me the parental love and care I had never had; they gave me a family! **The best part is, I know Jesus.** I was living in a dark cage, but **He used many people to rescue and restore me.** I believe that God had a plan for me from the beginning, and He allowed these things so I could testify that He is the one true God!

I am now a second-year college student pursuing a degree in Social Work. My dream is to bring change to my country in the area of Human Trafficking. Having gone through this bitter experience, I want to restore trafficking victims back into society and see sorrowful lives transformed to joyful ones.

My name is Pooja Ghimire. I'm 21. I've been living at Asha Nepal since I was 8.

My mother, Shoba, was from the same rural village in Nepal where I was born. She was the eldest of seven; when her father died, she and her mother raised the younger children. At 16 my mom married, and soon I was born, but when I was five months old, my dad married another woman for her dowry and left us without food or money.

Mother desperately struggled to care for me, but life was hard. I was very sickly. Just to survive, she left me with my father and his mother and returned to her own mother. Then a woman offered her a good job in a Kathmandu factory. That woman's "sister" arranged the trip and gave my mom some dry meat — it was drugged. She awoke as a slave, thousands of miles away in a Mumbai brothel — where she spent five miserable years in pain and darkness, without hope.

Meanwhile, I was also in severe distress. My cruel stepmother beat and threatened me, forced me to do all the housework and take care of my stepbrother. I had no education, proper food, or clothes, while my stepbrother did. I couldn't even remember what my own mother looked like.

My mom was finally rescued by the team from Bombay Teen Challenge, and went to Nepal to stay with Aunty Bimala at Asha Nepal. They formed a plan for rescuing me. When she came to my village, my stepmother hid me — she wanted to keep her slave. But one day my mom grabbed me and ran!

We fled to Asha Nepal. There I got everything I had been denied — good education, food, clothes — and lots of love and care.

At 9 I accepted Christ as my Savior. **All my painful experiences have helped me realize that God is there for me.** Jeremiah 29:11 became real to me: I know that God has a good plan for my life; whatever He does is to prosper me, to give me hope and a future.

I'm pursuing a degree in Business Administration, to become a banker and build my own business. I want to glorify God and encourage women who have gone through the same pain my mom experienced. I believe that God will help me achieve those dreams.

I am Savita Tamang, 25 years old; Asha Nepal has been my home for 10 years.

My mom was sold in India when she was very young. She became pregnant and sought an abortion, but my father said he would take full responsibility if the child was a boy. When I was born a girl, he refused to accept me. My mom was miserable; she had never wanted me in the first place. She sent me to various people who kept me for short periods. When I contracted polio, it became even harder to find someone to take me. Finally my mother paid a maid a large sum to take me, and I was raised in that family.

The woman's son and daughter-in-law abused me. They forced me to do household chores dawn to dusk even when I was seriously ill. I have the bitter memory of being hungry for long periods. Eventually they forced me to marry a very poor man who didn't even have a proper place to stay. But they lied to my mom, continuing to request money for my support.

When I refused to do what this man told me, he became violent. One day, he threw me out of the house. I was miserable. I went to stay with an aunt who had been trafficked to the brothel. She hid me in her place for three weeks, but knowing she couldn't protect me long, she begged for help from the Bombay Teen Challenge outreach team. They arranged my rescue. I asked them to help my mom too, and they were able to free her a few months later. We both were recommended to Asha Nepal — where we started our lives again.

My mom was with me for three years before she died. My family at Asha Nepal consoled me in my grief.

I wanted to utilize the beautiful life God gave me. At

107

school, I got good grades. I work at Asha Nepal as a caregiver for the children. Now I'm in my second year of college, studying Sociology. I'm working very hard: it's difficult after such a long gap in my education!

God has blessed me in many ways; **my dream is to be a good example for those who have lost hope and faith.** I also want a family of my own, and to lead a normal, happy life. God has proven to me that nothing is impossible in Him!

I am Ajay Pun Magar, and I'm 17. I've been living at Asha Nepal 11 years.

When I was young, my mother was taken from Nepal and sold into the brothel in India. From that time on, I lived with my uncle and aunty in Nepal. Those times were very hard for me. I was not sent to school; instead I was sent to work in the fields, to graze cows and goats. My mother did not forget me, though, and after a few years she arranged for me to come to India. I was sent to India and stayed with her for some years. I was still very young and unaware of the life my mother was suffering. Though I stayed with my mom, I was not given proper love and care. She seemed busy with her work all the time, unable to give me the attention I needed. I came under the influence of the bad people in the brothel, and I became a street kid, wandering here and there. Later on, I came to know about my mother's profession, and it made me very sad.

Fortunately after a few years, my mother and I were rescued by Bombay Teen Challenge and we went to Ashagram, the Village of Hope outside Mumbai.

I was very happy to arrive there. I felt like I had a really big family. Eventually, we were able to go back to Nepal, and we were sent to live at Shared Hope International's local partner organization, Asha Nepal, where I was even happier. Aunty Bimala was very supportive, loving, and caring. Unfortunately, my mother died in 2004. I was very sad and depressed. But again, I was loved by everyone, and they helped me overcome my sorrows. **I used to think I was alone — that nobody understood me, but God showed and reminded me of His promises** and always lifted me up when I was down.

Now, I have completed the 10th grade and am enrolled in a high school course in Hotel Management. In the future, I want to open a fine restaurant of my own and treat people with good food and service. But my dream is also to be a football player (which Americans call soccer). I play football for renowned clubs here in Nepal — and I am good at it! — so I want to utilize my talent and share the Gospel through sports ministry.

Nadine has begun a new life with our Shared Hope partner in Jamaica — a life she could never have imagined.

She never knew who her father was, and her mother lived with a very abusive man. In Jamaica, the family structure as we know it in America is almost non-existent. Eighty-five percent of children do not have a father's name on their birth certificate, and mothers do whatever they must to care for the children. This usually involves making an "arrangement" with a man who will help provide food or education in exchange for sex with the mother — and often with one or more of the children. They call it "making do."

Nadine was thrown out of the house for refusing her mother's boyfriend. Soon she had her own boyfriend and became pregnant. She was actually happy about this, because a girl who is not pregnant by the time she is 15 is looked down upon as a "mule." She went from boyfriend to boyfriend, and had a second child. But she couldn't take care of her children — and in desperation, she gave them to her mother. Nadine was deeply depressed; she saw no reason to live. In her despair, she sought God, whom she knew about but did not really know. Someone told her about Shared Hope's partner in Montego Bay.

Nadine now knows joy. Gaining work experience and being tutored a few days a week, she's learning to write and speak properly, so she can pass a course that will equip her as a housekeeper in the hospitality industry. She's also learning to make drapes and soft furnishings.

This young woman is enthusiastic about life-change. **The desire of her heart is to stop the cycle of violence, abuse, and immorality in Jamaica —** starting with her own family.

Across the island, in the vacation paradise of Negril, the Triple X club is the "happening spot" for tourists — and a place of misery for young women forced to entertain there. But Shared Hope's partner in Negril is training and educating young women in computer skills and cosmetology, providing accredited training for certification in the hospitality industry, and even sheltering girls fleeing life as a tourist's toy. Thanks to the support of Shared Hope's generous donors, these girls have opportunities that will keep them from falling prey in a country of limited opportunity.

Rekah wants it to be known she is not *from the brothel*. The brothel was simply a place she had to pass through on her way to a victorious life. It is a place that nearly devoured her and her children — and her hope, too. But it did not conquer her ... she conquered it — and left it behind forever.

Rekah's husband tried to kill both her and her precious Sunny and Payal with a butcher knife. She and the children fled, with just enough money to board a train to the city, but once they arrived at the tumultuous station in Pune, India, they had no place to go. For days they huddled in corners, begging for food, until a man told Rekah she could work in his chocolate factory. It was a deception that landed her with her children in Pune's brothels for four long years.

Shared Hope's partner in Pune befriended Rekah and eventually won enough of her trust to become legal guardians for her children. Then they built a relationship with the brothel owner, and eventually won Rekah's release.

Today, Rekah and her children are part of our partner's growing household of rescued women and children. Recently, generous friends like you helped Shared Hope supply them with an official yellow school bus, a requirement of the state for a private

Christian school. Rekah's children are excelling there — and Rekah recently received her diploma for completion of beauty school. She is now employed full-time as a hair stylist! Her dream is to earn enough to support herself and her children in their own home, and to give them the bright future they deserve.

Elsewhere in India, our long-time partner Bombay Teen Challenge continues to free women from the dark world of the brothels through the amazing and courageous work of their outreach teams. They are welcomed at Ashagram, our Village of Hope outside Mumbai, India.

Of all Shared Hope's partners, BTC is the most advanced in the higher education opportunities and vocational training it offers its residents, including dress-making, jewelry, and leather craft. Ties between BTC and Asha Nepal are strong. (Both Renu and Pooja's mother, Shoba, work as peer counselors at Ashagram.)

My name is Yvonne. My stepdad was my trafficker. He used me for pornography at five years old, then for sex, and then for sex with his friends. By 7, I was a runaway.

By 11 I had already been introduced to IV drugs on the street, a place that felt much safer than home. I kept trying to escape the torture, but there was literally no one to turn to. Once I told a police officer what was happening and begged him not to take me home … but he did just that. I realized then that no one would defend me and vowed to be the defender for my little sister and brother.

The night I saw my stepdad in my two-year-old sister's bed, molesting her, I realized the story I had told myself was a fantasy and that I had to get help. Eventually, some people came and took us all away and put us in separate homes.

I ran from foster care and spent a year on the streets squatting in vacant houses with other homeless kids. On my 13th birthday, a friend and I went to a park. To my horror, my stepdad was there, grabbed me, and this time locked me in the basement, where I was forced to service the men he brought in. I was 14 when I gave birth to a baby boy in that basement. And that is when anger and vengeance took deep root in my spirit.

I was put in a group home, my baby in a foster home. I ran immediately and was picked up by a guy who let me stay with him and bought me nice clothes, food, drugs. As long as I had sex with the men he brought — politicians, doctors, and others with expensive cars — I didn't get beaten. One night, a man violently attacked me — as I struggled for my life, I reached for the little knife I carried and stabbed him. There was no such thing as self-defense for a "prostitute." At 15, I was sentenced to adult prison for manslaughter.

I walked out five years later, alone and nowhere to go. I was in and out of jail, finally hitting bottom when I gave birth in prison and my daughter was taken from me. In the chapel, I wept and grieved for the first time ever, begging Jesus to restore me ... and the transformation began.

My climb out of the pit wasn't straight up, but day by day I got stronger. I began reading the Bible and going to a church where I met Linda Smith, who offered to train me in job skills at Shared Hope. During my time there, my daughter's father also became a Christian, and we were married.

A narrative that began with abuse, homelessness, drugs, sex trafficking, and prison has miraculously become a life story of restoration. My greatest joy? Reuniting with my husband, all my children, my mother and little sister and brother, and my foster parents. My only loss? Anger and vengeance. In their place is a thankful heart and a life of purpose.

I am a survivor of sex trafficking. More than that, I am an overcomer who, with the help of God, is standing on the rubble of my past.

My name is Jen. I was 8 when a new neighbor befriended me and other children on our street. He spoke kindly to us and became a familiar face, inviting us into his home when we got off the school bus. We knew about "stranger danger," but he was no stranger. He started giving us treats and money in exchange for taking our pictures. It didn't feel unsafe. He lived close enough that my mom could call me for dinner when she got home from work.

But then he began making us undress and then videotaping us. He forced us to do pornographic acts with each other, and then with adults that came to his house. He said if I told anyone, he would kidnap my little sister and kill my mother. When I left for school in the morning, I would kiss my mother good-bye, wondering if today would be the last time I'd see her. I would walk to the bus stop in terror because he would be sitting in his car across the street, reading a paper and watching my sister and me. Our bus stop was only three doors from my house — and we even had a crossing guard — but no one suspected something so terrible could be happening to us.

This horror finally ended after two years — when one day he was suddenly gone. But I was left with a lifetime of physical, emotional, and spiritual pain. Like other victims of child sex trafficking, every single day I struggle to hear God's voice over the accusing voices inside, to make meaning out of my dreadful past and to remember that I am not my story.

My destiny was brutally carved out for me, but gave me a powerful purpose. By sharing my story, I teach others what to look for. In my case, many people noticed something was wrong but didn't understand what they were seeing. My teachers decided I had a learning disability; my doctor saw but asked no questions.

I have finished nursing school; I'm studying to be a forensic nurse in child sex-trafficking cases. My goal is to teach medical professionals how to gently use therapeutic techniques in communicating with children such as I was, while preserving valuable evidence that will help bring their perpetrators to justice.

Indeed, I am not my story. I am a voice for those too scared to speak.

My name is Stephanie. On my 13th birthday I was invited to a party where a handsome older boy took an interest in me. After that, he seemed to turn up everywhere I went. I was convinced this was fate, and soon we began a relationship.

My mother worked day and night to support our family while my father was in Iraq. I had little supervision. This charming, older boy said he loved me and wanted to marry me; he bought me nice things and took me to nice places. However, in just a few months he demanded that I dance in a strip club. He was in a financial jam and needed my help.

It was degrading, but I did it "for us." Then he demanded I sell myself for sex. I refused, but he threw me out of the house on a bitterly cold night, telling me to make money or freeze. After a few hours of misery, I finally climbed into a car....

So began endless nights of selling myself to make the money my trafficker demanded. I descended into depression. I drank and took drugs to dull the pain. By 15, all I wanted to do was die. Police picked me up, recognized me as a reported missing child, took me home — but fearing what he would do if I didn't return, I ran back to my trafficker. Later I was arrested; as I was being put into the police car, I watched the buyer leave in his truck. I remember being so angry — how wrong! I am being arrested and he is driving away! I refused to talk and again was sent home on probation — where my trafficker came to get me, brutally assaulting me in front of my own house.

While I was hospitalized, my probation officer asked Linda Smith of Shared Hope to find a safe place where professionals had the skills to address my many needs. The closest such place was 3,000 miles away.

Sadly my story of seduction and exploitation is not unique. I saw victims as young as 10, and some much older, trapped since they were my age.

But the story of my restoration is unique. Shelters and services to address the needs of child sex-trafficking victims are scarce.

My journey has made me strong enough to be a voice for others. My faith in God and His way of making beauty from ashes has emboldened me to speak on their behalf. Funding for organizations like the ones that helped me is vital. The journey from victim to survivor and advocate — the journey I was able to take — depends on it.

IT'S MORE
THAN A LABEL ...
IT'S A LIFESTYLE

Calling on men to defend themselves, each other, and the women and children in their lives against the harms and horrors of the commercial sex industry.

• Invest in the children of America and the protection of their futures from predators involved in the commercial sex industry.

• Take a stand — declare that the sexual exploitation of women and children, using pornography, and buying sex is not something REAL MEN will tolerate.

It's the role men have been called to fill. It's a pledge worth making ... and one worth keeping. Being a Defender is living a life of integrity and purity. It's more than a label — IT'S A LIFESTYLE.

TAKE THE PLEDGE
BECOME A DEFENDER

VISIT THE DEFENDERS USA WEBSITE TODAY,
WWW.THEDEFENDERSUSA.ORG.
ENLIST IN THE CHALLENGE AND BE A
PROUD PART OF EFFECTIVE CHANGE.